THIS BOOK BELONGS TO

children's choice®

IF I OWNED A CANDY FACTORY

IF I OWNED A

Greenwillow Books

New York

CANDY FACTORY

by
James Walker Stevenson

pictures by
James Stevenson

Copyright © 1968 by James Stevenson
First published by
Little, Brown & Co. in 1968
New edition first published by
Greenwillow Books in 1989
Greenwillow Books, a division of
William Morrow & Company, Inc.,
105 Madison Avenue,
New York, N.Y. 10016.

First Edition
10 9 8 7 6 5 4 3 2 1

Library of Congress
Cataloging-in-Publication Data

Stevenson, James Walker.
  If I owned a candy factory/
  written by James Walker Stevenson;
  pictures by James Stevenson.
  p.   cm.
    Summary: A little boy plans the
  treats he would give his friends
  if he owned a candy factory.
    ISBN 0-688-08106-1.
    ISBN 0-688-08107-X (lib. bdg.)
    [1. Candy—Fiction.]
    I. Stevenson, James (date)
    II. Title.
  PZ7.S8475If 1989
  [E]—dc19

87-37581   CIP   AC

If I owned a candy factory, I'd write a letter to all my friends and ask them, "What kind of candy do you like best?" And, "What day is your birthday?"

Then,
on each person's birthday,
a car would pick him up.

On Harvey's
birthday
the car would
come and take
Harvey to my
candy factory.

"Happy
    birthday,
        Harvey."

Harvey and I would
go inside the factory.

"You said
gumdrops
in your
letter, didn't
you?"

"Yes."

"That's your gumdrop
collecting car,
Harvey."

"Oh, boy!"

Harvey and I
would ride
through my
factory

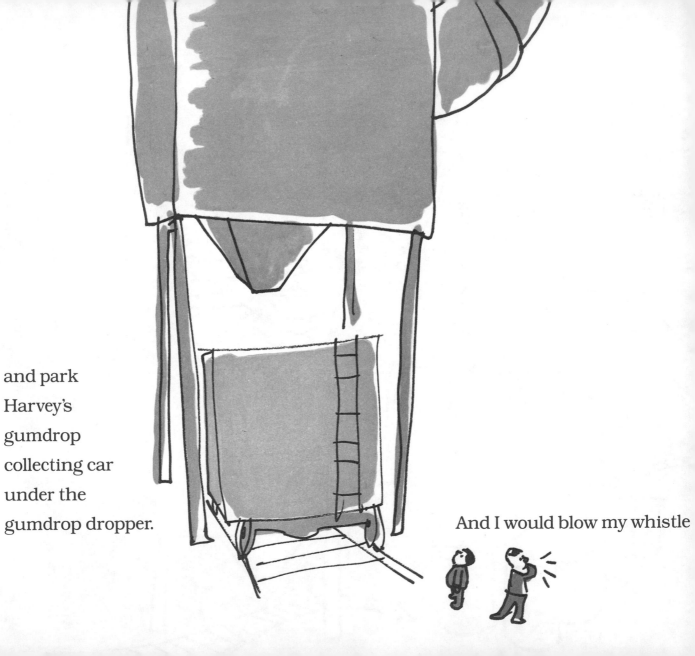

and park
Harvey's
gumdrop
collecting car
under the
gumdrop dropper.

And I would blow my whistle

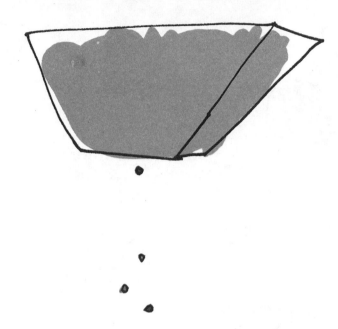

and down would come gumdrops

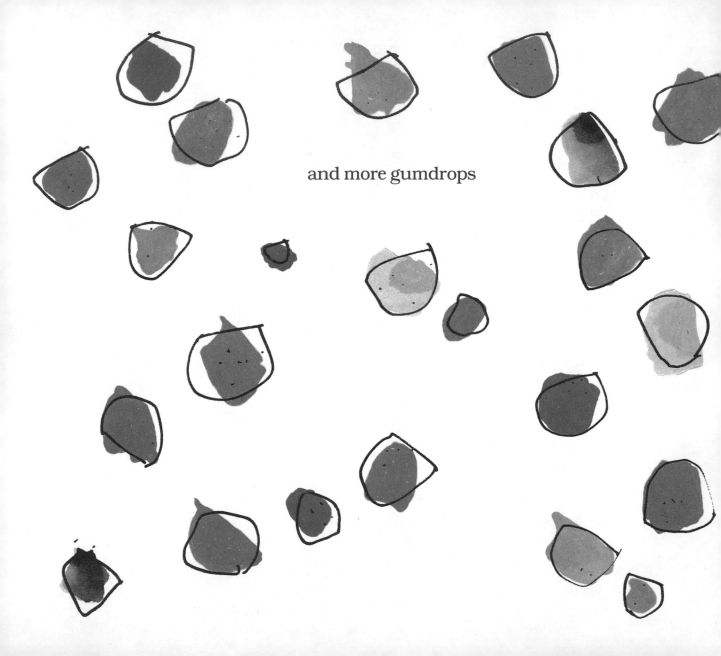

and more gumdrops

until the car was full.

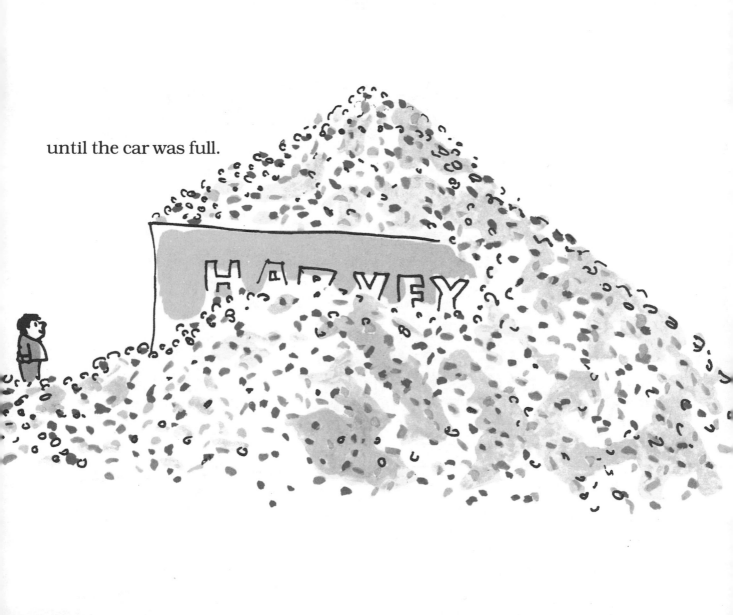

And then Harvey and his gumdrops
would get pulled home.

On Jane's birthday, the car would
pick her up and bring her to my factory.

Jane would say,  "Red lollipops, please."

And that's what she'd get.

On Peter's birthday

he would like

a very long string

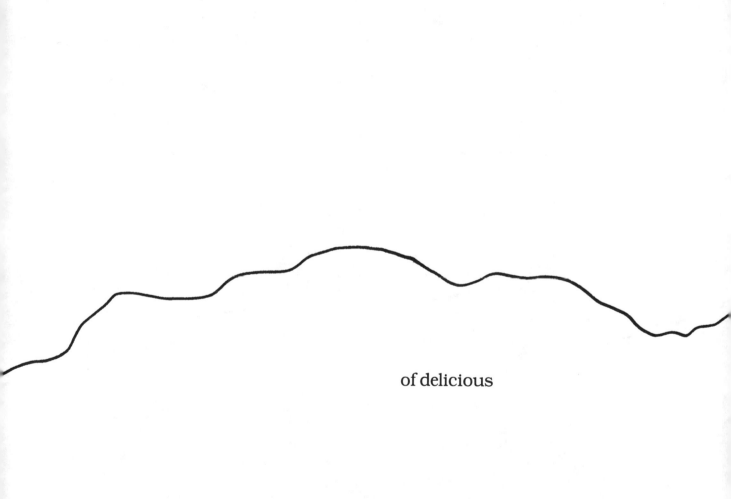

of delicious

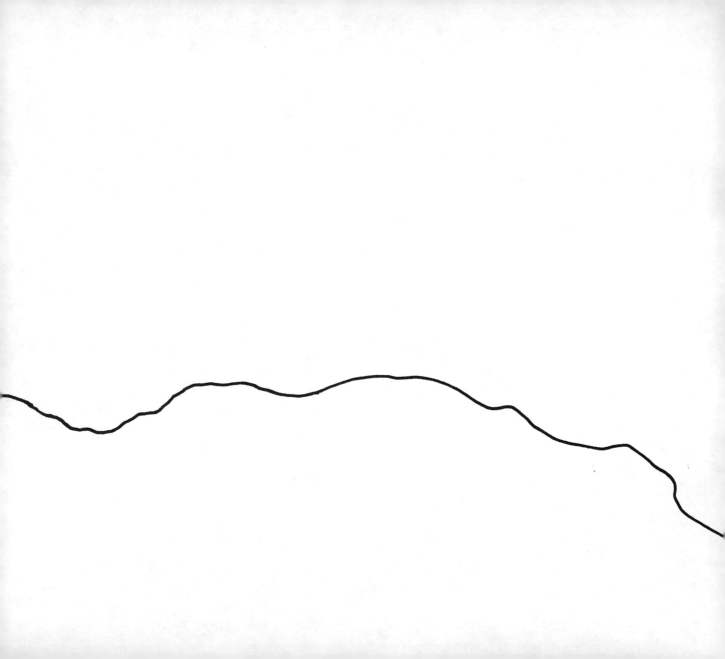

licorice.

After all my friends
had had their
birthdays and
taken their
candy home—

I would put
a big sign
on my factory

and I would invite

all the children
in the whole world

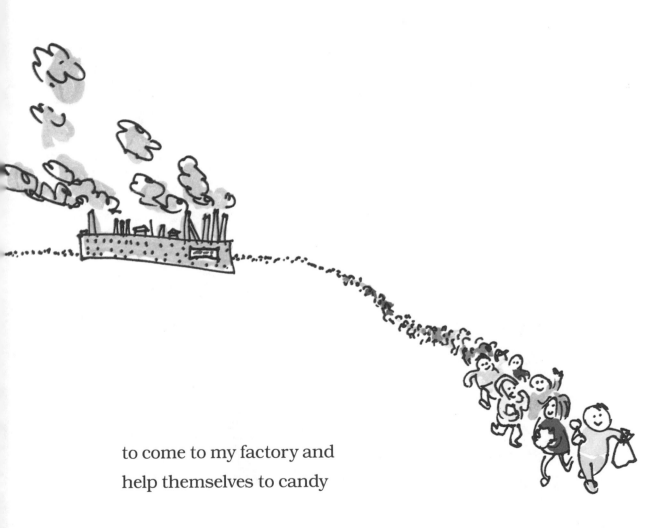

to come to my factory and
help themselves to candy

—if I owned
a candy factory.